DRINKING ANIMALS

Includes COCKTAIL RECIPES

COLORING BOOK

Get a free

BONUS
COLORING PAGE
by visiting
colormenaughtybooks.com/drinking

TABLE OF CONTENTS

In sequential order:

MOJITO

10 Fresh Mint Leaves
½ Lime, cut into 4 wedges
2 Tablespoons White Sugar, or to taste
1 cup Ice Cubes
1 ½ oz White Rum
½ Cup Club Soda

Place mint leaves and 1 lime wedge into a sturdy glass. Use a muddler to crush the mint and lime to release the mint oils and lime juice. Add 2 more lime wedges and the sugar, and muddle again to release the lime juice. Fill the glass almost to the top with ice. Pour the rum over the ice, and fill the glass with carbonated water. Garnish with the remaining lime wedge.

APPLE JULEP

2 oz. Cinnamon and Apple-infused Bourbon

½ oz. Rock Candy Syrup

½ oz. Fresh sweet and sour mix

Club soda

10 Fresh Spearmint Leaves

2-3 Thin slices of a red delicious apple

Muddle mint leaves with rock candy syrup and apple in the bottom of mixing glass. Add ice, bourbon infusion, sweet and sour mix and club soda to mixing glass. Gently rock back and forth to combine ingredients. Drop into a highball glass. Add additional ice as needed.

Garnish with a mint sprig.

Moscow Mule

9 Parts Vodka
1 Part Lime Juice
24 Parts Ginger Beer

Combine vodka and ginger beer in a highball glass filled with ice.
Add lime juice. Stir gently. Garnish with a wedge of lime.

MARGARITA

7 Parts Tequila
4 Parts Triple Sec
3 Parts Lime Juice

Rub the rim of the glass with the lime slice to make the salt stick to it. Take care to moisten only the outer rim and sprinkle the salt on it. The salt should present to the lips of the imbiber and never mix into the cocktail. Shake the other ingredients with ice, then carefully pour into the glass.

BLOODY MARY

3 Parts Vodka
6 Parts Tomato juice
1 Part Lemon juice
2 - 3 dashes of Worcestershire Sauce, Tabasco, Celery salt & Pepper

Stirring gently, pour all ingredients into highball glass. Garnish with celery and lemon wedge.

LONG ISLAND ICE TEA

½ oz Tequila
½ oz Vodka
½ oz White Rum
½ oz Triple Sec
½ oz Gin
1 oz Lemon Juice
1 oz Gomme Syrup
1 Dash of Cola

Add all ingredients into highball glass filled with ice. Stir gently. Garnish with lemon slice and sprig of mint. Serve with straw.

BANANA DAIQUIRI

1 oz Rum
3/4 oz Crème de Banane
Splash of Sour Mix
Dash of Simple Syrup
1 Banana

Blend all with a scoop of ice until smooth.
Garnish with fresh fruit.

COSMOPOLITAN

½ oz Fresh lime juice
1 oz Cranberry juice
½ oz Cointreau,
1 ½ oz Vodka Citron

Add all ingredients into cocktail
shaker filled with ice.
Shake well and double strain
into large cocktail glass.
Garnish with lemon peel.

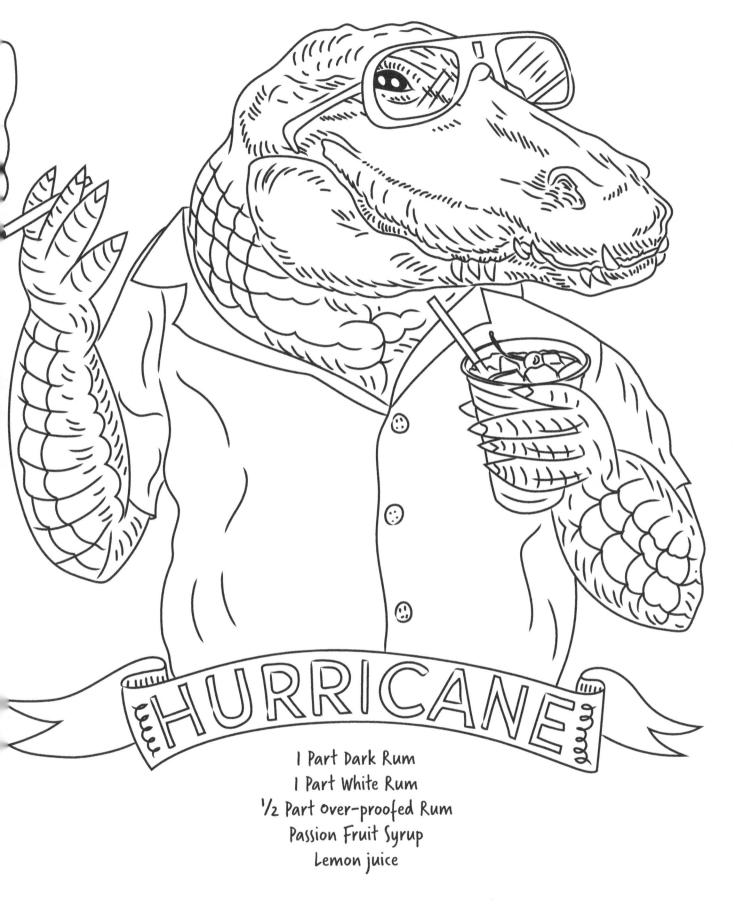

HURRICANE

1 Part Dark Rum
1 Part White Rum
½ Part Over-proofed Rum
Passion Fruit Syrup
Lemon juice

Shake ingredients with ice, then pour into a glass and serve over ice.

PISCO SOUR

3 Parts Pisco
1 Part Fresh Lime Juice
1 Part Simple Syrup
1 Egg White

In shaker with 5 large ice cubes (not crushed ice),
combine liquids adding egg whites last. Shake vigorously for 10-15
seconds. Strain into six ounce rocks glass (be careful not
allow any ice to pour into the cocktail.

B-52 BOMBER

⅔ oz Kahlúa
⅔ oz Baileys Irish Cream
⅔ oz Grand Marnier

Layer ingredients into a shot glass. Serve with a stirrer.

WHITE RUSSIAN

5 parts Vodka
2 parts Coffee liqueur
3 parts Fresh Cream
Pour coffee liqueur and vodka into an Old Fashioned glass
filled with ice. Float fresh cream on top and stir slowly.

EGG NOG

1 egg
2 Tablespoons sugar (for the yolk)
1 Tablespoon sugar (for the white)
a drop of vanilla

½ cup heavy cream
⅓ cup milk

Beat the eggs for 2 or 3 minutes with an electric mixer at medium speed until very frothy. Gradually beat in the sugar, vanilla and nutmeg. Turn the mixer off and stir in the cold brandy, rum, whipping cream and milk. Chill. To serve, sprinkle individual servings with more nutmeg.

CAIPIRINHA

2 ½ oz Cachaça
Half a Lime Cut into 4 Wedges
1 Teaspoons Sugar

Place lime and sugar into old fashioned glass and muddle (mash the two ingredients together using a muddler or a wooden spoon). Fill the glass with crushed ice and add the Cachaça.

HOT TOTTIE

1 Tsp. Honey
2 oz Boiling Water
1 ½ oz Whiskey
3 Whole Cloves
2 Cinnamon Sticks
1 Slice Lemon

Pour the honey, boiling water, and whiskey into a mug.
Spice it with the cloves and cinnamon, and put in the
slice of lemon.

GIMLET

5 Parts Gin
1 Part Simple Syrup
1 Part Sweetened Lime Juice

Mix and serve. Garnish with a slice of lime.

MANHATTAN

2 Parts Whiskey
1 Part Sweet Vermouth
1 to 2 Dashes Bitters, such as Angostura
Orange Peel
Maraschino Cherries

Place ice in a cocktail shaker. Add the whiskey, vermouth and bitters. Rub the orange peel
around the rim of the cocktail glass. Strain the drink into the glass.
Add 1 to 2 Maraschino Cherries.

PIÑA COLADA

1 Part White Rum
1 Part Coconut Milk
3 Parts Pineapple Juice

Mix with crushed ice in blender until smooth.
Pour into chilled glass, garnish and serve.

Gin Sour

1 1/2 oz Gin
1 oz Triple Sec
3/4 oz Lemon Juice
Add all ingredients into cocktail shaker filled with ice.
Shake well and strain into large cocktail glass.

GINGER
BEER
SHANDY

12 oz Chilled Ale
4 oz Ginger Beer

BELLINI

2 Parts Prosecco
1 Part Fresh Peach Purée
Pour peach purée into chilled flute, add sparkling wine. Stir gently.
Traditionally a Bellini uses white peaches for the fruit.

Made in the USA
Middletown, DE
24 November 2018